SCOTL [barcode]

D1193237

TRAVEL GUIDE

2022

Earth Voyage

TABLE OF CONTENTS

Welcome to Scotland
Scotland's Previews By Regions
Scotland's Essentials Top Sights

Welcome to Scotland

Scotland is a pleasure for those who know what they want since it is the ideal single malt. It is a heady blend of stunning landscapes and chic towns, salty sea air and ominous peat water, great outdoor activities, and fascinating history. Some of Western Europe's largest remaining wilderness areas can be found in Scotland. Golden eagles soar over the lochs and mountains of the northern Highlands in this wildlife paradise, where you may spot otters playing in the kelp along the coastlines of the Outer Hebrides and minke whales breaching through schools of mackerel off the coast of Mull. It's also a wonderland for adventure, where you can go hiking on the tundra plateaus of the Cairngorms, tightrope roping between the jagged peaks of the Cuillin, sea kayaking among the seal-inhabited islands of the Outer Hebrides, and taking a speedboat ride into the Corryvreckan whirlpool. Additionally, as it is a location that varies with the seasons, you will discover something fresh each time you visit. The bluebell-filled forests near Loch Lomond provide a violet haze in the spring. Due to their golden sand and turquoise water, the beaches in the Hebrides resemble those in the Caribbean throughout the summer. Perthshire's woodlands are a riot of autumnal hues in October and during the winter.

Strong heritage

Scotland has a lengthy and complicated history. A derelict croft on an island shore, a moor that was once a battleground, a beach where Vikings landed their boats, or a cave where Bonnie Prince Charlie hid are just a few examples of the many historical remnants that may be found throughout the entire country. Numerous castles, ranging from the unassuming yet frightening tower houses of Hermitage and Smailholm to the elaborately decorated strongholds of Caerlaverock and Craigmillar, demonstrate the nation's turbulent past. In locations like Bannockburn and Culloden, people commemorate and reenact conflicts that were crucial to the formation of a nation. Additionally, galleries and museums including the Maritime Museum in Aberdeen, Discovery Point in Dundee, and Kelvingrove in Glasgow highlight the contributions of Scottish engineers, artists, explorers, writers, and innovators to the development of the modern world.

However, tourists don't simply flock to Scotland's foggy beaches for the sake of history and adventure. Its restaurants no longer have a bad reputation for deep-fried food and unfriendly service, which is something that more and more tourists are discovering. Now, though, they offer food that rivals the best in Europe. Fresh fish that was captured just a few hours earlier, meat and venison that was raised just a few miles from your dining area, and organically grown veggies from your hotel's garden are all options. All of this is attributable to a growing esteem for top-notch regional cuisine. And to top it all off, sip on a rich, deep, and flavorful single malt whisky that is full of Scottish flavor.

West Highland Way

The best method to travel through Scotland's landscapes is by foot. know them. It's enjoyable to walk here even when it's windy, rainy, or swarming with flies. as a result of the numerous hills, short and long treks, and mountains. The Milngavie (near Glasgow) to Fort William (95-mile West Highland Way) Most hikers' dream destinations include Fort William. It is a arduous seven-day hike through some of the nation's top landscape that comes to an end beneath its tallest peak. Névis, Ben

Ben Nevis

Every year, some 100,000 people begin the summit trek, but only a small portion complete it. Still, the tallest Munro is climbable by anyone who is in reasonable shape. Ben Nevis will reward you with a stunning perspective and a terrific sense of success if you handle it with respect (if the weather is good). A fantastic method to prepare ready for a lengthy walk is to walk the 95-mile West Highland Way.

Glasgow

Although the largest city in Scotland lacks Edinburgh's timeless beauty, it more than makes up for it with a wealth of activities, kindness, and vibrancy that leave every visitor thrilled. It's an excellent location to view art galleries because it's contemporary and trendy. Despite being known for deep-frying Mars bars, it's also the best restaurant in Scotland. There is nothing left to do but live it when you combine that with what is likely the best pub culture in Britain and one of the top live music scenes in the world.

The Highlands

The far northwest is worth seeing, but there are many lovely views throughout the Highlands. The coast route between Durness and Kyle of Lochalsh offers breathtaking views at every turn, including the rugged Assynt Mountains, the serene serenity of Torridon, and the distant cape of Cape Wrath. Because of these qualities and the welcoming ambiance of the Highland pubs, this region of the country is difficult to forget.

The Isle of Skye

The most breathtaking scenery in a nation known for beauty can be found on the Isle of Skye. There are numerous locations to shoot shots, including the craggy Cuillin peaks, the Old Man of Storr and Quiraing pinnacles, and Neist Point's breathtaking seascape. Red deer and golden eagles can be spotted in the woods by walkers, and at the end of the day, they can refuel in welcoming pubs and upscale seafood eateries.

Edinburgh

Although the festivals in Scotland's capital are well-known, that is not all the city has to offer. There are many diverse moods in Edinburgh. The Old Town can be seen silhouetted against a blue spring sky and a golden haze of daffodils if you visit out of season. A warm glow may be seen emanating from a pub's window on a chilly December morning as rain falls on the cobblestones and fog clings to the spires of the Royal Mile.

Loch Lomond

The bonnie banks and bonnie braes of Loch Lomond, made famous by one of Scotland's most well-known tunes, are one of the most picturesque locations in the nation despite being only about an hour's drive from the busy city of Glasgow. The first national park in Scotland is where the loch is located. It is a large lake in the south with islands and bluebell woodlands lining its margins. It becomes more condensed and resembles a fjord in the north, where 900-meter mountains surround it.

Scotland's Castles

Numerous castles in Scotland reflect the country's stormy history and its contentious relations with its neighbor to the south. These castles range from lonesome stone strongholds that loom in the mist to majestic castles that tower over ancient cities and opulent palaces constructed on expansive grounds by lairds who were more concerned with luxury than protection. A ghost is rumored to prowl the corridors of most castles, and most of them have a tale (or ten) about schemes, intrigues, imprisonments, and betrayals.

Perthshire

Salmon leap upstream to the location of their birth, noble trees blanket the hills, gorgeous glens pierce through distant wildness, and blue-gray lochs sparkle as the weather changes. In Perthshire, a county in the center of the nation, sheep graze on fields that appear to be unnaturally lush and charming towns are bursting with flowers. There is a sense of the abundance of nature there that is unique to Scotland.

Marine Animals

Scotland is one of the best locations in Europe to witness marine life. Numerous cruise companies on the west coast nearly guarantee that passengers will see minke whales and porpoises during the peak months of July and August. The bottlenose dolphins that dwell year-round in the Moray Firth are well-known. Basking sharks, the largest fish in British waters with a maximum length of 12 meters, are also frequently sighted. Both Tobermory and Easdale, which are close to Oban, are excellent departure points.

Scotland's Previews By Regions

Edinburgh

The Scottish capital is a city of high culture and high ideals, as well as fine art, literature, philosophy, and science. It has been dubbed the "Athens of the North." This is where the largest arts festival in the world takes place every summer, rising like a phoenix from the ashes of its stellar reviews and box office records to usher in a brand-new round of accolades. The city's numerous theaters, top-notch art galleries, and museums offer much to see and do even when the festival isn't going on. Scottish history has benefited greatly from Edinburgh Castle. It is perched atop a shadowy rock with a view of the city's core. As the city expanded from its medieval Old Town to its elegant Georgian New Town, so did Scottish nationalism. The city's top-notch museums and historic structures display the evolution of both the city and the Scottish nation. The most stunning and enigmatic church in Scotland, Rosslyn Chapel, is located on the outskirts of the city.

Edinburgh

Glasgow

Glasgow has a rich history of trade, industry, and education, which has resulted in an impressive array of museums and art galleries, led by the magnificent Victorian cathedral of culture, Kelvingrove, which has so many diverse things to see that it can be difficult to know where to start. The nightlife of Glasgow is the liveliest in all of Scotland, from its famed trendy bars to its classic Victorian pubs. With numerous venues and musicians, including both established international acts and up-and-coming Scottish bands, it is also the hub of the live music scene in Scotland. With its well-known structures and interiors by Charles Rennie Mackintosh, majestic Victorian architecture in the city's core, fashion boutiques in the Italian Center, and design exhibits at the Lighthouse, Glasgow aspires to be the most fashionable city in Scotland.

South Scotland's

Rolling hills and deserted abbeys make up Scotland's southern border. The gothic ruin sites of Melrose, Jedburgh, Dryburgh, and Sweetheart, as well as the fortified Hermitage Castle, Caerlaverock Castle, and Smailholm, reveal much about a turbulent past. The best Adam-designed mansion in this region is Dumfries House, a time capsule of Chippendale architecture, along with Culzean Castle, Paxton House, Floors Castle, and Mellerstain House. Although the granite hills of Galloway and Arran are fantastic for hill walking and the 7stanes trail centers have some of the greatest and most difficult mountain riding in the UK, the rounded, heather-covered hills of the Southern Uplands cannot match the grandeur of the Highlands.

Central Scotland's

Because St. Andrews' Old Course is the oldest course in the world and Scotland is the country where golf originated, every golfer aspires to play there. The game is administered by the Royal & Ancient Golf Club, which was established in 1754. Over 600 years have passed since the game was first played here. From the charming seaside towns along Fife's coast to the forested lochs and hills of the Trossachs, central Scotland features all the traditional Scottish scenery. As well as the magnificent mountain landscape of Glen Lyon and Glenshee, it features the enormous trees of Perthshire. Although some claim that Stirling's castle is the best in the nation, other noteworthy castles include Scone Palace, Blair Castle, Kellie Castle, Doune Castle, and St. Andrews Castle.

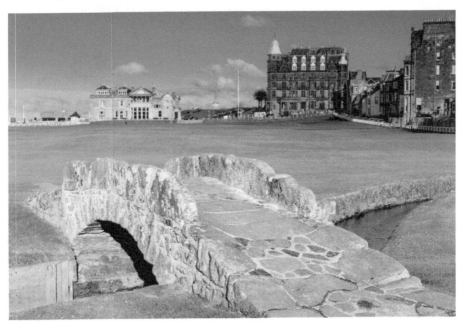

Central Highlands

The Cairngorms' Aviemore and Fort William both have a ton to offer in terms of outdoor entertainment. Whether you wish to cycle the paths surrounding Loch Morlich, hike the West Highland Way, climb Ben Nevis, or ski the Cairngorm slopes, there is something for everyone. Photographers will adore Glen Coe's untamed splendor and the Cairngorms' snow-capped peaks. They will also adore the golden beaches and island views of Arisaig and Morar, as well as the Caledonian pine forests that surround Loch Aric. The most well-known Scottish legend, the Loch Ness monster, claims to reside here. The Great Glen and the Culloden battlefield are both worthwhile visits even if you don't see Nessie.

North Highlands

The northern Highlands and islands are the very core of Scotland, a wilderness of sea and mountains that continues to be one of Europe's most pristine locations. From the peaks of Assynt and Torridon to the jagged rock pinnacles of the Cuillin Hills to the brilliant beaches of the Outer Hebrides. Hikers, cyclists, climbers, and kayakers may take advantage of the Northwest's abundance of open space to go on excursions and view some of the UK's most stunning species. The northern abandoned settlements, particularly Arnol Blackhouse and the Skye Museum of Island Life, are excellent resources for learning about the Clearances.

South Highlands

This region is home to some of Scotland's most stunning wildlife, including the white-tailed sea eagles at Mull and the minke whales and basking sharks that cruise the west coast. A beaver that had been extinct for hundreds of years was also introduced back into the wild there. One of the best ways to see the western coast is to travel from island to island, and this collection of islands - Islay with its whisky distilleries, wild and mountainous Jura, picturesque Mull and the little jewel of Iona, and the gorgeous beaches of Colonsay, Coll, and Tiree - is a great place to start. One of the best things about the area is the quantity of seafood, regardless of whether you eat at a top restaurant in Oban or Tobermory or if you eat with your fingers on the harborside.

Shetland & Orkney Islands

These islands are bordered by coral reefs but lack any vegetation. Their prehistoric settlements, cemeteries, and stone circles are distinctive, and they have an intriguing Viking history. Maes Howe is among the best Neolithic tombs in Britain, while Skara Brae is the best-preserved prehistoric settlement in northern Europe. Both were constructed before Egypt's pyramids. Because of the abundance of gannets, fulmars, kittiwakes, razorbills, puffins, and Europe's largest Arctic tern colony in the summer, Shetland is a fantastic area to see birds. On Unst, Scotland's farthest northmost inhabited island, there is a wildlife preserve called Hermaness.

Scotland's Essentials
Top Sights

Edinburgh

It's plenty of odd places that make you want to keep wandering, from the vaults and wynds (small lanes) of the Old Town to the urban towns of Stockbridge and Cramond. And every time you round a curve, you see something unexpected: a glimpse of rust-red cliffs, a flash of blue sea in the distance, or green hills lighted by the sun. However, there are other activities besides sightseeing in Edinburgh. There are fantastic stores, eateries, and bars. Pub crawls and spontaneous jam sessions, wild clubbing, all-night celebrations, binge eating, late nights, and early morning stroll through cobblestone streets are all common occurrences in this city. During the festival in August, when it feels like the entire world has descended upon Edinburgh for one giant celebration, all of these wonderful things come together. You should join them if you can.

The best places to visit in Edinburgh are the city's core, the Royal Mile in the Old Town between the castle and Holyrood, and the New Town. One notable exception is the Royal Yacht Britannia. It is located around two miles northeast of the city center in Leith's renovated docklands neighborhood. You can simply stroll around Stockbridge and Morningside, the charming riverside village of Cramond, the winding trails of Calton Hill, and Arthur's Seat if you grow weary of visiting attractions.

Royal Mile

1. Edinburgh Castle

Edinburgh is a result of Castle Rock's ominous shadows, which rise over Princes Street's western end. Along the invasion route between central England and central Scotland, this rocky hill was the simplest to defend. Numerous armies, including the Roman legions in the first and second centuries AD and Bonnie Prince Charlie's Jacobite soldiers in 1745, had traveled this road. Edinburgh Castle has played a significant role in Scottish history as a royal residence and a fortress. The first time it was inhabited was in the 11th century by Queen Margaret and King Malcolm Canmore (who reigned from 1058 to 1093) In 1745, the stronghold was last utilized during hostilities. It served as the primary British army base in Scotland from that point on until the 1920s. It is currently one of Scotland's most fascinating, well-liked, and pricey tourist destinations. On either side of the Entrance Gateway are statues of William Wallace and Robert the Bruce. It connects to a cobblestone lane that ascends beneath the Portcullis Gate from the 16th century and leads to the Argyle and Mills Mount batteries' cannons. The battlements here provide a fantastic perspective of New Town and the Firth of Forth.

The renowned One O'Clock Gun, located at the far end of Mills Mount Battery, is where spectators congregate to watch a gleaming WWII 25-pounder fire an audible time signal at precisely 1 pm (every day save Sunday, Christmas Day, and Good Friday). The road turns to the left past Foog's Gate and up to Castle Rock, where the tiny Romanesque St. Margaret's Chapel, Edinburgh's oldest structure, is located. This is located south of Mills Mount. It was most likely constructed in the early 1100s in memory of their mother, Queen Margaret, who was canonized in 1250. Most likely, David I or Alexander I constructed it. Most of the structures on Castle Rock's summit are gathered around Crown Sq, where the Scottish National War Memorial stands out. On the other side lies the Great Hall. James IV, who reigned from 1488 to 1513, had it constructed as a location for celebrations. The Scottish parliament utilized it up until 1639. The most intriguing feature of it is the original hammer-beam roof from the 1600s. The Castle Vaults, located beneath the Great Hall and accessible through the Prisons of War exhibit in Crown Square, have been used as bakeries, storage facilities, and even prisons at various points throughout history. A prison from the early 18th or 18th century has been recreated in the vaults. You may read writing from French and American prisoners on the antique wooden doors.

The Royal Palace, which dates from the 15th and 16th centuries, is located on the east side of the plaza. The best feature of the castle is a strongroom that houses the Honours of Scotland, the oldest royal jewels remaining in existence in Europe. It is reached after a series of historical episodes. The crown, sword, and scepter were put away in a chest after the Act of Union in 1707 and left forgotten until they were rediscovered in 1818 by the author Sir Walter Scott. The crown was constructed in 1540 using the gold from Robert Bruce's coronet from the 1400s. The Stone of Destiny is also visible in this location. The apartment where Mary, Queen of Scots, gave birth to her son James VI, who would reign both Scotland and England simultaneously in 1603, is close by in one of the Royal Apartments.

2. St Giles Cathedral

Most of High St. is taken up by the enormous, gray structure known as St. Giles Cathedral. The patron saint of cripples and beggars, St. Giles, is honored by the name St. Giles Cathedral. Only from 1633 to 1638 and from 1661 to 1689 was it a true cathedral, housing a bishop. Here is where a Norman-style church was erected in 1126. Invaders from England demolished it in 1385, leaving just the tower's supporting central piers standing. The existing church was largely constructed in the 15th century. The crown spire, for instance, was completed in 1495. But a lot of it was updated in the nineteenth century. Although the interior is not particularly large, it is highly historical. The Scottish Reformation was centered at St. Giles, where John Knox served as the pastor from 1559 to 1572. The Thistle Chapel was erected in 1911 by the Knights of the Most Ancient and Most Noble Order of the Thistle. It is among kirk's most fascinating features. The 16 knights' helmets and arms are intricately carved onto the canopies of the gothic-style stalls. Among the vaulting, keep an eye out for the angel playing the bagpipes. Outside St. Giles' western door, on the cobblestones of the roadway, is a sculpture called The Heart of Midlothian. The toll booth used to be located here.

Built in the 15th century and destroyed in the early 19th century, the Tolbooth. It served as a venue for meetings of the General Assembly of the Reformed Kirk, the municipal council, and parliament. In addition, it served as a courthouse, a prison, and a location for executions. For good luck, people frequently spit on their hearts (don't stand downwind!). The Mercat Cross, a reproduction of the original 1365 structure where traders and merchants gathered to conduct business and where royal announcements were given, is located at the opposite end of St. Giles.

3. Holyroodhouse

While Mary, Queen of Scots lived there in the 1600s, this palace serves as the official residence of the Scottish royal family. Holyrood Abbey's guest house served as the palace's first tenant. King James IV added to it in 1501. The oldest remaining portion of the structure is the northwest tower. It was constructed in 1529 as a royal residence for James V and his wife, Mary of Guise. Six turbulent years of Mary, Queen of Scots' reign were spent here. She fought with John Knox during that time, wed her first and second husbands, and saw the murder of her secretary David Rizzio. When the royal family is there and when there are state events (often in mid–May and mid–June to early July; consult the website for exact dates), the palace is off limits to the general public. The self-guided audio tour concludes in the Great Gallery after taking you through a number of stunning royal rooms. The 89 portraits of Scottish monarchs that Charles II ordered are claimed to demonstrate his uninterrupted descent from Scotia, the Egyptian pharaoh's daughter who discovered Moses in a reed basket on the banks of the Nile. The Bed Chamber, where Mary, Queen of Scots lived from 1561 to 1567, is the highlight of the visit. A covert staircase leads from there to her husband's sleeping chamber.

Here, the pregnant queen was restrained by her envious first husband, Lord Darnley, as his men beheaded the queen's beloved secretary, Rizzio. Where he bled to death is noted on a plaque in the following room.

4. Scotland's National Museum

The majority of the broad, elegant Chambers St. is taken up by the National Museum of Scotland's lengthy front. It contains two buildings, one modern and one Victorian, and there are many interesting things to see there. Major repairs and renovations took place over a two-year period, and the museum reopened to the public in 2011. The museum's new structure, which debuted in 1998, is a well-known landmark in the area. It boasts remarkable modern architecture and is constructed of golden stone. The museum's five levels display Scotland's historical development from the time of the dinosaurs to the 1990s. There are many imaginative and fascinating exhibits, and audio guides are offered in a variety of languages. The 1861-built old Victorian museum is attached to the modern structure. The old museum's drab facade gives way to a light-filled space with a glass canopy. Natural history, archaeology, scientific and industrial technologies, and ornamental arts from ancient Egypt, Islam, China, Japan, Korea, and the West are just a few of the diverse treasures housed in the museum.

Glasgow

The largest city in Scotland has evolved over the last few decades to rank among the most intriguing cities in all of Britain. It now features a deceptive blend of upscale and commonplace characteristics. Modern bars, excellent restaurants, and a hedonistic party scene surround its Victorian structures, satiating your midnight whims. Glasgow has one of the best live music scenes in all of Britain. There are numerous locations where local beats can be heard. The great industrial and cultural history of the city is creatively displayed in the city's various museums and art galleries. Charles Rennie Mackintosh's artwork is everywhere in the town, and the River Clyde, which once represented the gritty side of the city, is now a symbol of its rejuvenation. Glasgow residents take great pride in their Marxist traditions, working-class heritage, and dark sense of humor. Glasgow is a mesmerizing blend of fashion, urban edge, and the renowned kindness of its residents.

Glasgow's top sights are very evenly dispersed. Many of them are located along the Clyde, which is the focus of a long-term campaign to rebuild the neighborhood, in the East End's cathedral district, and on the South Side, which is home to many museums. The majority of museums are free. The center also has a ton of attractions, particularly Mackintoshania. Students abound in the hip West End throughout the academic year.

1. Glasgow Herald's

The Glasgow Herald's stunning new home was housed in Mackintosh's first structure, which was constructed in 1893. The Scottish Centre for Architecture & Design is now there. It is located on Buchanan St. up a small path. It also features the Mackintosh Interpretation Centre, which provides a thorough (if a little dry) account of his life and work, as well as a number of temporary displays that are quite technical and occasionally require admission. The rooftops and spires of the city center may be seen clearly from the top floor of the "lighthouse."

2. The Municipal Council

The stately City Chambers were established as the heart of municipal administration in the 1880s, when the city was at its wealthiest. The interior is much more lavish than the exterior, and the chambers have been utilized in films to represent the Kremlin or the Vatican. Free tours are conducted at 10:30 a.m. and 2:30 p.m. Monday through Friday. The Royal Highland Fusiliers Museum depicts the history of the Royal Highland Fusiliers and other regiments from 1678 to the present. The walls are covered in uniforms, medals, photos, and other military mementos. The wrought ironwork was created by Mackintosh.

3. Glasgow Cathedral

Glasgow Cathedral is one of those uncommon places that feels as though it has always been there. The gloomy, towering interior evokes the power of the Middle Ages and can send chills down your spine. It is a stunning example of Gothic architecture, and unlike almost all of Scotland's cathedrals, it escaped the Reformation mobs relatively unscathed. The majority of the structures we see now were constructed in the 1500s. A side door leads into the nave, which is decorated with regimental flags hung from the ceiling. The wooden roof on top has been repaired numerous times since it was first constructed, although some of the wood dates back to the 14th century, as evidenced by the superb shields. The cathedral's stunning, slender stained-glass windows are mostly recent. The west window is occupied by Francis Spear's 1958 work The Creation. The cathedral is divided into two sections by a late-15th-century stone choir screen. The two halves are then embellished with seven pairs of figures depicting the seven deadly sins. There's a choir over there. The four stained-glass pieces depicting the Apostles in the east window are particularly poignant. Francis Spear also created them. The upper chapter house, where Glasgow University was founded in the 15th century, is accessible from the northeast corner. There is now a sacristy there.

The bottom church is the cathedral's most interesting section. It is accessible by stairs. Its pillar forest provides an eerie ambiance around St. Mungo's tomb. (In the fifth century, St. Mungo established a monastic community here.) This tomb was the focal point of a well-known medieval pilgrimage that was regarded to be as wonderful as visiting Rome. The necropolis behind the church ascends and descends a magnificent green slope. The city's wealthy manufacturers' magnificent Victorian tombs make for an interesting walk, great views, and a faintly Gothic thrill.

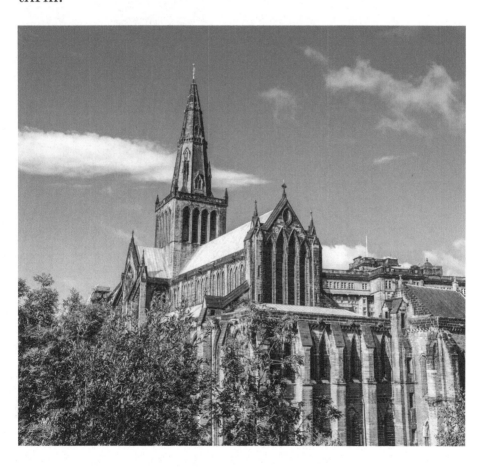

Glasgow Cathedral

4. Science Centre Glasgow

The most significant millennium project in Scotland is the ultramodern Glasgow Science Centre. Children of all ages will be occupied for hours by it. There are numerous interactive exhibits that bring science and technology to life on each of its four floors. Beware of the illusions, such as the 3-D head scan that rearranges your appearance and the cloud chamber that displays natural radiation. The museum is made up of a floor-to-ceiling windowed interactive Science Mall and an egg-shaped, titanium-covered IMAX theater. This is a fantastic location for young, inquisitive minds to learn a lot. A 127-meter rotating observation tower, a planetarium where the Scottish Power Space Theatre brings the night sky to life, and a virtual science theater where guests can embark on a 3-D molecular adventure are all present. To reach here, take the First Glasgow bus 89 or 90 from Union St. or the Arriva bus 24 from Renfield St.

North Scotland

Many people rush right by this region of the country on their way to popular tourist locations like Loch Ness and Skye. But by doing so, they are skipping over a part of Scotland that is just as beautiful and diverse as the more popular tourist attractions in the west. The Discovery, Captain Scott's research ship for the Antarctic, is based in Dundee, the city of jute, jam, and journalism. Aberdeen is a granite metropolis and an industrial powerhouse supported by the wealth of North Sea oil. Within Scotland's borders are these two of the country's four largest cities. The majority of Scottish Baronial castles in the nation are located in Aberdeenshire and Moray, along with hundreds of distilleries around the River Spey. Rich in agriculture, Angus is home to stunning glens and mystery stones that the ancient Picts left behind.

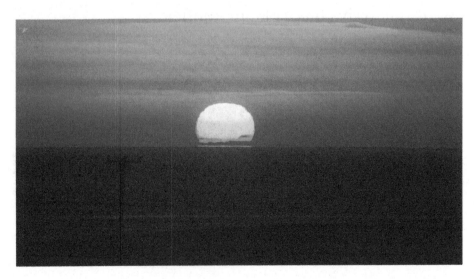

DUNDEE & ANGUS

Angus is a thriving agricultural area that extends from the Highland border up to the north of Dundee, the fourth-largest city in Scotland. The broad valleys (straths) and low, green hills that define this lovely region stand in stark contrast to the rich, reddish-brown soil of recently tilled farms. The gorgeous shoreline stretches from the lengthy, sandy beaches at Montrose to the red-sandstone cliffs of Arbroath. The Grampian Mountains' foothills are punctuated by romantic glens, and the coastline is dotted with miles of sandy beaches. This area was the Pictish kingdom's administrative hub in the seventh and eighth centuries, and it is still home to a large number of intriguing Pictish sign stones. With a few notable exceptions, such as the crowds that visit Discovery Point in suddenly self-assured Dundee and the coach loads that traipse through Glamis Castle, Angus is a sort of tourism backwater and a good place to escape the crowds.

1. Dundee

Nelson is honored with a statue atop his column in London's Trafalgar Square, Sir Walter Scott is honored with a monument on Princes Street in Edinburgh, and Queen Victoria is seen in front of Belfast's City Hall. On the other hand, a bronze monument of Desperate Dan graces City Square in Dundee, giving the place a charming touch. One of the most popular animated characters is Dan from the children's comic book The Dandy, which has been released by the DC Thomson company in Dundee since 1937. He is well-known to multiple generations of British schoolchildren. Dundee has what is possibly the best location of any Scottish city as it sprawls along the northern side of the Firth of Tay. Additionally, the city is home to Discovery Point and the Verdant Works museum, two tourist destinations that are regarded as having national significance. It is evident that Dundee is well worth a visit when you take into account the quaint beach town of Broughty Ferry, Dundee's vibrant nightlife, and the people of Dundee itself, who are among the warmest, most welcoming, and most entertaining people you will ever experience.

Dundee

Discovery Point

Along the riverside to the south of the city's core, the three masts of Captain Robert Falcon Scott's renowned polar expedition ship, the RRS Discovery, can be clearly seen. The ship's wooden hull was at least half a meter thick when it was built in Dundee in 1900 to ensure its survival in the pack ice. It sailed for the Antarctic in 1901 and spent both of those winters locked in place there. Beginning in 1931, it was laid up in London, where its condition deteriorated further until it was saved in 1925 by the efforts of Peter Scott (Robert's son) and the Maritime Trust. The ship was given a berth at her home port of Dundee in 1986, and it quickly became a representation of the resurgence of the city there. The ship itself, which is docked in a secure harbor and is visible from all sides, is the main attraction. There are galleries and video exhibits in the main structure that provide a fascinating history of both the ship and the Antarctic research. You may take tours of the bedrooms Scott and his crew stayed in, as well as the ship's bridge, galley, and mahogany-paneled officers' wardroom. Discovery Point and the Verdant Works can both be accessed with a single ticket, which costs £13.50 or $8.50 per adult or child, respectively.

McManus Galleries

You can explore everything there is to see at the McManus Galleries without feeling hurried or overloaded because it is a city museum on a small scale. They are located in a substantial Victorian Gothic building that Gilbert Scott built in 1867. The exhibits, which span the city's history from the Iron Age to the present day and cover the full time period from the Iron Age to the current day, include artifacts from the Tay Bridge Disaster and the Dundee whaling business. The Sinclair ZX81 and Spectrum, both of which were produced in Dundee in the early 1980s, will appeal to computer enthusiasts. They were cutting-edge personal computers with a full 16K of RAM.

2. Angus

The names of five charming glens that may be found slicing into the highlands along the southern boundary of Cairngorms National Park are Isla, Prosen, Clova, Lethnot, and Esk. The northern and southern regions of Angus are divided by the Grampian Mountains. The most breathtakingly beautiful glens, according to some, are Glen Clova and Glenesk, but Glen Lethnot receives the fewest tourists. However, each of the glens has its own qualities and beautiful scenery. You can learn more about the many hikes that are offered in the Angus Glens at the tourist information center in Kirriemuir and at the Glen Clova Hotel in Glen Clova. There is no additional public transit available to the Angus Glens other than a restricted school bus service along Glen Clova; for more information, contact the visitor centers in Kirriemuir or Dundee.

GLEN ISLA

At the bottom of the valley, close to the Bridge of Craigisla, is Reekie Linn, a stunning waterfall. Reekie, which translates as "smoky" in Scottish, gets its name from the cascading spray that pours from the falls. The waterfall rises 24 meters. You can walk another five miles to reach the higher, wilder parts of the glen after reaching the end of the road in Auchavan. The Caenlochan National Nature Reserve is located on the high plateau and was created to protect the unusual alpine flora.

GLEN PROSEN

On Tulloch Hill (380m), which is situated about six miles north of Kirriemuir at the base of Glen Prosen, there is a pleasant forest walk that leads to the Airlie monument. About a mile before Dykehead, on the eastern road, the trip starts. From Glenprosen Lodge at the top of the glen, a nine-mile journey along the Kilbo Path over a pass between Mayar (928m) and Driesh (947m), then descends to Glendoll Lodge at the top of Glen Clova (allow five hours).

Central Scotland

The history of Scotland's central region is significant. The landscape is dotted with significant castles and ruins from the region's past. The Stone of Destiny was used to crown monarchs in Perth, the old capital, and significant wars fought in Stirling altered the path of Scottish history. The Lowland belt gives way to the splendor of the Highlands as travelers travel north from Glasgow and Edinburgh, giving them a feel of the country as a whole. With deep, dark, steely-blue lochs that, on quiet days, reflect the shadows of tall, rugged peaks like sentinels, Scotland's landscape is at its most stunning here. Whether you're in the big-tree country of Perthshire, the desolate lands of Glenshee, or the verdant coast of Fife with its fishing communities, there are various ways to take in the scenery. You can go for a walk, a bike ride, or a mountain climb. Additionally, the region offers some of the top bars and eateries in the nation, where weary travelers can go at the end of the day.

1. STIRLING

This region, which makes up Scotland's wasp-like waist, has long served as a crucial strategic crossroads between the Lowlands and the Highlands. Because of Stirling's high fortress, is why the two pivotal battles for Scottish independence were fought here. Scotland became a country after the victories of William Wallace at Stirling Bridge and Robert Bruce at Bannockburn, which occurred 17 years apart. The region still holds a lot of pride for many people in the nation. The castle at Stirling is one of the most fascinating in all of Britain, and the Old Town is perched at a stunning height. The enchanting Trossachs, where Rob Roy resided and where Walter Scott found inspiration, are accessible. The Old Town of Stirling is a treasure trove of stunning structures and cobblestone lanes leading up to its imposing castle's ramparts, from which you can view for miles. It is perched on a sizable wooded crag that is the remnant of a long-gone volcano. It's simple to spot The Wallace Monument, a peculiar Victorian Gothic structure dedicated to the well-known liberation fighter from the Braveheart film. The nearby town of Bannockburn is where Robert the Bruce defeated the English in a significant battle.

While the castle is great to visit, you should also take some time to stroll through the Old Town and along the lovely road that circles it. The Old Town in Stirling is more charming than the shopping-centric modern Stirling. You'll adore it here if you hang out as high as you can.

2. Stirling Castle :

Scotland is under your hands if you can hold onto Stirling. Since the Stone Age, this proverb has ensured that there has been some sort of fort present. You can't help but compare Stirling's fortress to Edinburgh Castle, yet due to its setting, design, historical significance, and commanding vistas, many people think it is more fascinating. Due to the high number of people, it is preferable to visit in the afternoon. By 4 p.m., you might have the castle to yourself since most visitors just stay for the day.(www.historic-scotland.gov.uk; adults: £13, children: £6.50; 9.30 am to 6 pm, October through September; 5 pm, March)
The present castle was constructed between the late 1400s and the 1600s, during the reign of the Stuart rulers. The nicest aspect of a vacation is without a doubt the stunning Royal Palace, which was recently renovated. In order to impress James V's new French bride and other European kings and queens, it was intended to appear brand-new, just as it did when it was constructed by French masons under his direction in the middle of the 1600s. The six-room suite is a riot of color and has three rooms for the king and three for the queen.

The stunning fireplaces, the meticulously crafted tapestries that have been carefully woven over many years, and the ceiling of the king's audience hall with its replica painted oak discs are particularly noteworthy. These prints are based on the originals, which are housed in the Metropolitan Museum in New York. They depict the unicorn chase, a distinctly Christian event. Don't overlook the Stirling Heads Gallery, which is located above the royal chambers, or the lovely sculptures on the palace's exterior. This has the original oak roundels, which represent a who's who of historical royalty, courtiers, and notable figures. In the cellars below the palace, there is a children's exhibit on castle life. The huge Great Hall, which James IV constructed, the Royal Chapel, which James VI renovated at the beginning of the 17th century, and the King's Old Building surround the main castle courtyard. The Royal Chapel still preserves the vibrant original mural painting. The Museum of the Argyll & Sutherland Highlanders is now located here; admission is free, but donations are welcome. From 1794 until 1854, the museum chronicles the history of this illustrious regiment, notably its illustrious defense in the Battle of Balaclava in 1854. Read the letters from the World Wars if you can. They stir the soul.

Until the last tapestry is finished, which is likely by the end of 2013, you can observe the weavers at work at the Tapestry Studio at the far end of the castle. Watching it is pretty cool. The Great Kitchens, which demonstrate how busy and large it was to prepare food for the king, as well as the Castle Exhibition, which is located close to the entrance and provides up-to-date information on ongoing archaeological digs, are additional exhibits. The views from the ramparts are breathtaking. The admission price includes a free audio guide, and free tours depart often from a location close to the entrance. For an additional £2, or for no charge if you are a member of HS, tours also proceed to Argyll's Lodging at the summit of Castle Wynd. Scotland's most remarkable townhouse from the 17th century is this lovely lodge. Even turrets are on it. The renowned author William Alexander, Earl of Stirling, once lived there. It displays how affluent people lived in the 17th century and has been nicely restored. There are just four or five daily trips available for entry.

STIRLING CASTLE

3. Stirling Old Town

The steep Old Town, just below the castle, has a very different vibe from contemporary Stirling. Architectural marvels from the 15th to the 17th centuries can be found throughout its cobblestone streets. When Stirling became a royal town (about 1124), it began to expand, and in the 15th and 16th centuries, wealthy merchants began to construct residences there. The best remaining town wall in Scotland is in Stirling. It was constructed about 1547, the year Henry VIII of England launched the "Rough Wooing" by attacking the town in an effort to compel Mary, Queen of Scots, to wed his son in order to unite the two kingdoms. A nice route to view the wall is via the Back Walk, which runs beside it from Dumbarton Road to the castle. You pass the town cemeteries on your way there, where you may see the enormous Reformation symbol known as the 1863 Star Pyramid. The route continues around the castle's exterior to Gowan Hill, where you can see the Beheading Stone, which is currently enclosed by iron bars to prevent modern-day use. The elaborate façade of a Renaissance townhouse known as Mar's Wark may be seen on Castle Wynd, which is at the top of Old Town. The wealthy Earl of Mar, who served as Scotland's regent when James VI was a toddler, erected it in 1569.

STIRLING

4. DUNBLANE

Dunblane, a lovely town with a well-known cathedral, is located 9 kilometers north of Stirling. It's difficult not to remember the horrific massacre in the elementary school in 1996, but better headlines have recently come the town's way as a result of the emergence of local tennis star Andy Murray. Dunblane Cathedral (High Street; www.dunblanecathedral.org.uk; Cathedral Square; free admission; 9:30 a.m. - 5:00 p.m.) Mon–Saturday, 2-5 pm Sun From April to September, from 9.30 a.m. to 4 p.m. on weekdays and from 4-6 p.m. on weekends. During those months, I took a detour to observe the Sun (Oct.–Mar.) It is a superb Gothic sandstone edifice with a clever design. The lower sections of the walls were built during the Norman period, while the remaining portions were mostly built during the 13th and 15th centuries. The bell tower, on the other hand, was built next to an ancient structure dating back to the 12th century. A carved Celtic stone from the 10th century stands at the top of the nave, while a standing stone in town commemorates the children who were slaughtered. Just a few meters away from the cathedral is the musty ancient Leighton Library (www.leightonlibrary.co.uk; 61 High St; free admittance; 11 am–1 pm; closed Sun).

The oldest private library in Scotland, which dates back to 1684, is open Monday through Saturday from May to September. There are almost 4500 books available in 90 different languages. If you use Darn Road, which was originally used by monks, it will take you around an hour to walk from Dunblane to Bridge of Allan. Furthermore, trains and buses run frequently between Stirling and Dunblane.

5. DOUNE

Doune can be found on the way to Callander, not far down the road from Dunblane. Visit Doune Castle (HS; www.historic-scotland.gov.uk; adult/child £5/3; 9.30 am-5.30 pm Apr-Sep, to 4.30 pm Oct-Mar, closed Thu-Fri Nov-Mar), one of the best-preserved 14th-century castles in Scotland. It was the royal family's favorite hunting lodge, but it also had strategic importance because it commanded the roadway that connected the Lowlands and the Highlands. Mary, Queen of Scots, as well as Bonnie Prince Charlie, stayed here. Throughout his reign, Bonnie Prince Charlie used it to detain government forces. The castle walls provide some of the best views in the area, and the lofty gatehouse, which rises roughly 30 meters, is a sight to behold. It's probable that some people will know the castle from Monty Python and the Holy Grail. Doune is around 12 kilometers north of Stirling. The First (www.firstgroup.com) bus service operates at a reduced frequency on Sundays than on other days of the week.

DOUNE

6. Trossachs region

Because of its spectacular natural beauty and good walking and cycling pathways that are conveniently positioned close to the major population centers of the south, the Trossachs region has long been a favored weekend getaway destination. Its status as a national park means that its allure will not fade anytime soon, thanks to its densely forested hills, stunning lochs, and an ever-expanding selection of unique places to eat and stay. The Trossachs gained appeal as a tourist destination in the early nineteenth century, thanks to Walter Scott's poem "Lady of the Lake," which was inspired by Loch Katrine, and Rob Roy, which was about the daring-do of the region's most famous son. Visitors arrived from all around the country, captivated by the poetry's romantic language. Even while the Trossachs can become congested with coach tours during the summer, the vast majority of these people are only there for the day, so calm, leisurely nights spent watching the reflections in the nearest loch are still possible. It is recommended that you schedule your travel so that it does not fall on a weekend.

Trossachs

South Scotland's

Even though many people are aware of how beautiful southern Scotland is, many people simply drive by it on their way to northern Scotland. Big blunder. However, it does imply that there is space to breathe and peaceful areas here in the summer. There were raids and conflicts because southern Scotland was so near to England. There was a lot of fighting at the bleak border fortifications. There was loot to be had in the Borders, where powerful, affluent abbeys presided over rural communities. These buildings were frequently broken into before being demolished during the Reformation. Their remains, which are linked by biking and walking pathways, are among the most intriguing historical monuments in Scotland. There are several woodlands between the major market towns in the hillier west. The hills tumble down to sandy sections of seashore with some of Scotland's best weather. It's the home of Robert Burns, whose poetry demonstrated how down-to-earth he was and how much he enjoyed socializing. Arran is a picturesque island that is ideal for trekking, riding, and sightseeing.

1. The Borders

The Borders is a one-of-a-kind location. Hundreds of years of fighting and plunder have left a scarred landscape encircled by the ruins of the great Border abbeys. Their richness was an enticing pull during the Border Wars, and they were destroyed and rebuilt numerous times. The monasteries burned destroyed in the 1600s and were never rebuilt. These massive stone shells are now the best thing to see in the neighborhood. But it isn't all. Friendly communities with historic customs can be found in the countryside. On the coast, you'll find one of Europe's best sites to dive in cold water, as well as majestic homes just begging to be explored. Because the rolling slopes contain so many different colors of green, it's also an excellent spot to hike or ride a bike. Also, don't miss Hermitage Castle, which is the greatest spot to learn about the area's difficult history.

Peebles

Peebles is one of the prettiest Border towns. The town's main street is located on a ridge between the River Tweed and the Eddleston Water. Even though there aren't many attractions, you'll want to remain for a few days due of the pleasant ambiance and fantastic walking trails in the neighboring wooded hills. If the weather is nice, the walk along the River Tweed provides plenty of grassy spots for picnics and a playground for children (near the main road bridge). A mile west of town, Neidpath Castle is a tower house perched on a blu above the river. It's currently closed, but it's worth a look from the river.

Melrose

Melrose is a little town that thrives thanks to tourism. Melrose is situated at the foot of the three heather-clad Eildon Hills. It has a traditional market square as well as one of the big abbey ruins. The red-sandstone Border Abbey is possibly the most intriguing of the major Border abbeys. Melrose Abbey was destroyed twice by the English in the 1400s. The ruins are noted for their exquisite stonework, and the cracked shell that remains is pure Gothic. Look up to see if you can spot the pig gargoyle playing the bagpipes on the roof. You'll have a magnificent view if you climb to the summit. David I established the abbey in 1136 to house Cistercian monks from Rievaulx Abbey in Yorkshire.

2. Selkirk

Selkirk was a thriving mill town in the early 1800s, but it now stands peacefully and picturesquely atop its high ridge. The river valleys below Selkirk were most likely previously noisy with machinery. For 30 years, Sir Walter Scott was the sheri of this area. They would have had to face a terrible mill worker in court if he had broken the law. Halliwell's House Museum is located inside the oldest structure in Selkirk, which was built in 1712. Admission is free. The museum features an intriguing display about local history, and the shows at the Robson Gallery next door rotate. Stop into Sir Walter Scott's Courtroom (Market Square; free admission Mon–Sat 11 a.m.–3 p.m. Apr–Oct) to see an exhibition about his life and writings, as well as an intriguing story about the brave explorer Mungo Park, who was born near Selkirk, and his search for the River Niger.

3. Hawick

Hawick, which is located on both sides of the River Teviot and is pronounced "hoik," is the largest town in the Borders and has long been a prominent center for knitting. There are numerous large businesses in town where you may get sweaters and other woolens.

The three buildings that comprise "The Heart of Hawick" are located in the heart of the town. The famous Drumlanrig's Tower, a stone mansion that used to be the primary home of the Douglas clan, sits on the other side. It is now the Borders Textile Towerhouse, which illustrates the story of knitwear manufacturing in the town. The Heritage Hub is a cutting-edge structure. Anyone interested in learning about their Scottish ancestors or browsing other local archives is welcome to visit.

4. HERMITAGE CASTLE

Hermitage Castle (www.historic-scotland.gov.uk; adult/child £4/2.40; 9.30 am-5.30 pm Apr-Sep), commonly known as "The Strength of Liddesdale," is a symbol of the Scottish Borders' terrible history. Because it is vacant and proud, with large squared-o stone walls, it appears to be a refuge for orc-raiding groups rather than a house for Scottish nobles. It is one of the most heartbreaking and moving Border ruins. The castle was strategically vital, and it was where many horrible things happened and filthy deals were struck with the English invaders. All of this backfired on the unscrupulous Scottish lord in the issue. In 1338, Sir William Douglas imprisoned Sir Alexander Ramsay, a man he disliked, and purposefully starved him to death. Ramsay survived for 17 days by eating grain that fell from the granary above and into his trench, which is still visible today. In 1566, Mary, Queen of Scots, famously went to see Lord Bothwell, who was injured and staying in the castle. He grew stronger, murdered (possibly) her husband, married her, and then abandoned her after a few months and fled. The castle is around 12 miles south of Hawick on the B6357.

HERMITAGE CASTLE

5. Jedburgh

Countless old buildings and wynds (narrow alleys) have been tastefully restored, making Jedburgh a pleasant place to stroll around. It's constantly crowded with Americans, but if you walk down some of the charming side streets, you can hear a pin drop. (www.historic-scotland.gov.uk; Abbey Rd; adult/child £5.50/3.30; 9.30 a.m.-5.30 p.m., April-September; 9.30 a.m.-4.30 p.m., October-March) The government took over Jedburgh Abbey, the first of the great Border abbeys, and it shows. There are audio and video exhibits throughout the meticulously preserved ruins that tell the narrative of the monastery (good for the kids). The red sandstone ruins lack a roof but are otherwise in decent condition. Some of the exquisite (but deteriorated) stone carvings in the nave demonstrate how skilled the master mason was. In 1138, David I established the abbey as a residence for Augustinian canons.

Jedburgh

THE END

Made in the USA
Coppell, TX
11 September 2022